A is for Algonquin

An Ontario Alphabet

Written by Lovenia Gorman and Illustrated by Melanie Rose

Sleeping Bear Press

310 North Main Street, Suite 300
Chelsea, MI 48118
www.sleepingbearpress.com

© 2005 Thomson Gale, a part of the Thomson Corporation.

Thomson, Star Logo and Sleeping Bear Press are trademarks
and Gale is a registered trademark used herein under license.

Printed and bound in Canada.

10 9 8 7 6 5 4 3 2 1

Library of Congress Cataloging-in-Publication Data

Gorman, Lovenia.
A is for Algonquin : an Ontario alphabet / written by Lovenia Gorman;
illustrated by Melanie Rose.
p. cm.
Summary: "This A to Z children's pictorial covers Ontario's famous people,
history, geography, and provincial symbols. Topics include Alexander Graham
Bell, Eastern White Pine, Group of Seven, James Bay, and Niagara Falls. Each
letter's topic is introduced using poetry and includes expository text filled
with details about the topics"—Provided by publisher.
ISBN 1-58536-263-8
1. English language—Alphabet—Juvenile literature. 2. Ontario—Juvenile
literature. I. Rose, Melanie, ill. II. Title.
F1057.4.G67 2005
971.3—dc22   2005007468

To my children, Alexandra and Sawyer, and to my husband, Andrew—
thank you for inspiring me through my writing process.

To my family—thank you for your support and encouragement.

To Heather Hughes, Jan Napier, and Aimee Jackson of Sleeping Bear Press—
thank you for this wonderful opportunity. Dreams really can come true.

LOVENIA

To my friend, Lisa, from Uxbridge, Ontario.
Thank you for everything.

MELANIE

From "A" to "Z"
cover to cover.
Let's explore Ontario
there is "More to Discover."
Heartland of Canada is its name.
Let's learn all about Ontario—
its beauty and its fame.

A a

Located in central Ontario, Algonquin Provincial Park is a huge area of forests, rugged ground, and fresh water. Canada's oldest provincial park was established in 1893 in order to preserve the land in its natural form and to manage the commercial uses of the park. The best way to explore Algonquin is by canoe or foot. Its 1,500 kilometres of canoe routes and peaceful backpacking trails make Algonquin Park a great getaway for many, all year long. Summer is the most popular time to visit the park. Many families come to camp, fish, and paddle the many lakes, hoping to see a moose, deer, or wolf along the way. In winter, visitors explore the park by snowshoe or dogsled.

Ontario has 104 operating provincial parks. Besides Algonquin, other popular parks in our province include Bronte Creek, Killarney, Quetico, and Wasaga Beach.

A is for Algonquin Park,
    a popular camping ground.
Hike, canoe, or snowshoe—
        it's fun here all year round!

The letter **B** is for a man
whose invention we know well.
We can talk on the telephone
thanks to Alexander Graham Bell!

Alexander Graham Bell came to live in Brantford, Ontario with his family in 1870. He first thought of the idea for the telephone while visiting his family home in Brantford during 1874. Two years later he invented the telephone. While the first recorded phone conversation happened in Boston in 1876, the first long-distance telephone call was placed between Brantford and Paris, Ontario on August 10th of the same year. During this call Bell heard his Uncle David say, "To be or not to be…" over the telephone. The Bell family home became a Canadian National Historic Site in 1953.

B also stands for Frederick Banting and Charles Best, who made the discovery of insulin at the University of Toronto between 1921 and 1922. This discovery has saved the lives of many people who have been diagnosed with diabetes. Their finding is considered to be the most important Canadian contribution to medicine.

C c

C is for the Canadian Shield
that stretches far and wide.
Rivers, forests, and tundra
cover most of our countryside.

The Canadian Shield is the largest
physical region in Canada, covering
two-thirds of Ontario. The rivers in the
region flow toward the Great Lakes,
Hudson Bay, or the St. Lawrence River.
In between the rocky landforms and
rivers are marshy lands called muskeg.
The northern part of the shield is
covered with tundra, or frozen ground.
A variety of wildlife lives in the area
such as beaver, moose, caribou, and
deer. The Canadian Shield is one of
the world's richest areas in natural
resources. Many minerals are mined
here, especially in Ontario. The largest
and best known mining town is
Sudbury, Ontario. Since the Canadian
Shield is such a large area that con-
tains many mineral deposits, mining
is one of Canada's largest industries.

During 1929, DeHavilland Aircraft of Canada began building airplanes at a small airfield in Downsview, Ontario. As years passed, the airfield was enlarged to allow jet fighters of the Royal Canadian Air Force to use the site. World War II brought growth to DeHavilland. The company expanded from 35 workers in 1939 to over 7,000 employees by 1945. At this time the company was building one to three planes a day. When the second World War ended, the company became private and began to build planes that were suitable to Canada's severe climate. Some of these planes included the very famous Chipmunk, Beaver, and Otter, which were sold in Canada and throughout the world. Today the Bombardier/DeHavilland Company continues to use the airfield at Downsview for testing and delivering airplanes. It is here where the Dash 8 is produced, assembled, and sold worldwide.

The DeHavilland Aircraft Company begins with the letter D.
Building planes for the world to fly, let's learn its aviation history.

Dd

E e

The Eastern White Pine became our provincial tree on May 1, 1984. It is easily grown in a variety of soil types and found throughout Ontario. The Eastern White Pine is the tallest coniferous tree in eastern North America, growing 30 to 50 metres tall.

Our provincial tree is a valuable resource. It has been traded as softwood lumber in Ontario for hundreds of years. Since it is one of the faster growing evergreens, the Eastern White Pine has been used for reforestation projects, landscaping, and Christmas trees.

The Eastern White Pine tree is our provincial tree. It grows throughout Ontario and it starts with the letter E.

Old Fort William in Thunder Bay is the world's largest recreated fur trading post. Today visitors can explore the fort and inland headquarters for the North West Company, North America's leading fur trading company, just as it was in the early 1800s. Characters in historical costumes participate in activities that echo the past, as they take you back in time to when the fort operated as a fur trading post.

Other historical forts are located throughout Ontario. Some of these include Old Fort York in Toronto, Fort George in Niagara-on-the-Lake, and Fort Henry in Kingston. All three of these forts were used during the War of 1812 to protect British waterways from American invasions.

F also stands for the Provincial flag of Ontario. On May 21, 1965, it became the province's flag. Its red background is decorated with the Union Jack, the provincial shield, the Cross of St. George, and three gold maple leaves.

Ff

Old Fort William is for F. Journey back into the day when traders met to swap their goods near a place called Thunder Bay.

G is for the Group of Seven,
  Tom Thomson in the lead.
Their artwork of Algonquin Park
  is outstanding, it's agreed.

Tom Thomson was the artist who inspired the painters who eventually formed the Group of Seven. J. E. H. MacDonald, Arthur Lismer, Fredrick Varley, Frank Johnston, Franklin Carmichael, A. Y. Jackson, and Lawren S. Harris were the seven artists who formed the original group. Many of these artists first met when they were working together in Toronto.

Thomson encouraged his artist friends to join him on sketching trips to Algonquin Park. Tom Thomson discovered how light reflected on northern landscapes and the bright colours of autumn when sketching in Algonquin. A Georgian Bay cottage belonging to a friend of the artists also became a preferred sketching place for the men.

After the mysterious death of Tom Thomson in 1917 and the end of World War I, Algoma, Ontario became a favourite location for the artists to paint. In 1920 the artists began to call themselves the Group of Seven. The group developed a new belief that Canadian art must be inspired by the land of Canada.

H is for Henry Hudson,
who discovered Hudson Bay.
He sailed through northern waters
dodging ice along the way.

In 1609 Henry Hudson, a British explorer, crossed the Atlantic Ocean to North America hoping to find the Northwest Passage to Asia. While doing so, Hudson and his crew sailed up a river, now known as the Hudson River, named after the explorer. The river brought Hudson to a large body of water which he thought was the Pacific Ocean. In reality, Hudson and his crew had discovered the body of water known today as Hudson Bay. During the winter they explored what is now called James Bay and became trapped here in the ice. When spring arrived, the crew feared that Hudson would want to continue searching for the Northwest Passage so they put Hudson, his son, and other members who supported him in a small boat and sailed away. Hudson and his men were never seen again.

H also stands for the Heartland Province, Ontario's nickname. It is called this because it is located toward the interior of Canada.

I is for the Islands
　　　dotting the lake and seaway too.
When boating in eastern Ontario
　　　a thousand will surround you.

The Thousand Islands are located throughout the St. Lawrence River and the eastern shores of Lake Ontario between Canada and the United States. On the Canadian side the islands extend from Wolfe Island near Kingston, Ontario, to the Brockville narrows at Brockville, Ontario. In reality there are more than 1,800 islands in the area, ranging in size from very small to large islands with docks and waterfront homes. The islands are said to be one of the most beautiful places to visit in Ontario. Cruise boats tour the Thousand Islands from various towns in the area and offer a variety of activities to tourists. A good view of some of the islands can be seen from Kingston, Ontario.

I also stands for other Ontario islands, such as Pelee Island, a popular destination for bird-watchers, or Toronto's Centre Island. To learn more about Manitoulin Island, see the letter **W**.

Ii

From late June to early September of every year, the Polar Bear Express takes visitors to Ontario's north on a unique and exciting tour by train. Beginning in the town of Cochrane, passengers travel approximately 300 kilometres to Moosonee in the James Bay Lowlands. The train follows the same path taken by the earliest explorers to Canada's north. The four and a half hour train ride is said to be one of the greatest rail excursions in the world. While aboard the train passengers can view the isolated forests, lakes, and muskeg areas of the north. Tourists will see historic fur trade posts and rivers such as the Abitibi and Moose rivers along the way.

Take a unique adventure and discover the choice for J. The Polar Bear Express will take you to Ontario's north: James Bay.

Jj

The Kincardine Scottish Festival and Highland Games take place every July in Kincardine, Ontario. Competing pipe bands and tossing of the caber are two of the many events that can be enjoyed throughout the day.

On every summer Saturday evening, the world-famous Kincardine Scottish Pipe Band Parade takes place. This pipe band is one of the oldest and largest in Ontario. The band parades throughout Kincardine as it invites visiting pipers and drummers to take part in this popular summer tradition.

K also stands for Kitchener-Waterloo, where many Pennsylvania Mennonites came to settle in Ontario in the late eighteenth century. Some Mennonites still have strict values and use traditional farming methods today as they continue to live in rural, community-based environments. Kitchener-Waterloo also has a large German community. The German heritage is celebrated every fall through popular Oktoberfest events.

Kincardine Highland Games begins with the letter **K**.
Learn many Scottish traditions when you visit for a day.

The Common Loon was named the provincial bird on June 23, 1994 by the Ontario Legislature. The loon is a water bird that can be found swimming on many of Ontario's rivers and lakes. It is well known for its eerie, lonely call and its excellent swimming abilities. Cottagers often hear loons across lakes during summer evenings in areas such as the Muskoka district of our province.

The Common Loon is also found on the Canadian dollar coin. The coin is nick-named the "loonie" because of the loon featured on its face.

L also stands for London. In 1854 London became a city. The city was named after London, England. It is often referred to as the "Forest City" because it is located in an agricultural region of Ontario. London is also home to the University of Western Ontario.

L1

Loon begins with the letter L—
it is our provincial bird.
Listen closely and from across the lake
its eerie call is heard.

M m

When he was five years old Sir John A. Macdonald and his family moved to Kingston, Upper Canada. He became interested in politics at an early age. Sir John A. Macdonald was the most important Father of Confederation. His role in Confederation led him to become the first prime minister of Canada on July 1, 1867. Macdonald helped to form Canada as a nation through the development of the transcontinental railway. The Canadian Pacific Railway united Canada from coast to coast and encouraged the development of the west. Macdonald remained in office until November 5, 1873. He was reelected on October 17, 1878. His time as prime minister ended with his death on June 6, 1891.

M also stands for the Muskoka District of Ontario. This popular cottage area includes Georgian Bay, Muskoka Lakes, Huntsville, Bracebridge, Gravenhurst, and Lake of Bays. The area is rocky, heavily treed, and includes over 1,600 lakes.

M is for Sir John A. Macdonald
from Kingston, we can boast.
The first prime minister of our country
uniting us from coast to coast.

N is for Niagara Falls,
its water thunders down.
A Natural Wonder of the World
attracting visitors year round.

Located in southern Ontario is the seventh Natural Wonder of the World, Niagara Falls. It is one of the world's most popular travel destinations. Over 15 million visitors come to see the falls yearly. Niagara Falls is split into two falls, the American Cascading Falls in New York and the Canadian Horseshoe Falls in Ontario. Approximately 155 million litres of water flow over the falls every minute! This water comes from four of the Great Lakes. Once it reaches the falls, the water flows down the Niagara River to Lake Ontario. It then travels along the St. Lawrence River to the Atlantic Ocean. Most of the water from the falls is used for creating electric power in North America, making Niagara Falls the largest producer of hydroelectric power in the world!

N also stands for James Naismith, the inventor of basketball. Naismith was born in Almonte, Ontario. In 1891, using peach baskets and a soccer ball, Naismith created "basket ball."

N
n

Four of the five Great Lakes border Ontario: Lakes Erie, Huron, Superior, and Ontario. Lake Ontario is the smallest of the Great Lakes in surface area. Found at the base of Niagara Falls, Lake Ontario has many beautiful rural resorts. The shores of the lake have some large urban centres located along it, like Hamilton. Originally named Lake St. Louis in 1632, it was renamed by the Iroquois in 1660, its name meaning "beautiful lake."

Lake Erie is the shallowest and warmest of the Great Lakes. The southernmost point on Canada's mainland, Point Pelee National Park, is found on Lake Erie.

Lake Huron is the second largest Great Lake in surface area and the fifth largest freshwater lake in the world.

Lake Superior holds 10 percent of the world's freshwater and is the largest freshwater lake in the world by surface area. The lake could hold all of the other Great Lakes plus three more lakes the size of Lake Erie!

O o

One of the five Great Lakes
is the choice for O.
Its beauty is in its name
for our Lake Ontario.

The place for **P** is Parliament Hill,
found in Canada's capital city.
Ottawa has the Peace Tower
and gardens that are pretty.

Pp

Located in Ottawa, Canada's capital city, Parliament Hill is where Canada's laws are made. Canada's members of Parliament work in the Parliament Buildings. The parliament, or government of Canada, includes the Queen, represented by the Governor General, the appointed Senate, and the elected House of Commons. The Prime Minister of Canada, who is the leader of the House of Commons, also works in the Parliament Buildings. The Parliament Buildings are located near the Ottawa River in downtown Ottawa. The Centre Block building is where the Peace Tower is found. It was built to commemorate the end of World War I and stands in the centre of Parliament Hill. Free tours of Parliament Hill are offered year-round. Special festivals and ceremonies attract many tourists. In the spring visitors come to see the spectacular gardens on Parliament Hill that display thousands of tulips during the Canadian Tulip Festival.

Q can be for Queen's Park
where the legislature resides.
MPPs from across the province
make important decisions inside.

The legislature at Queen's Park is located in Toronto. It is here where our Members of Provincial Parliament, or MPPs, meet from across the province to discuss important issues, make decisions, and pass laws for all Ontarians.

Canadian citizens living in Ontario who are 18 years or older have the right to vote and elect MPPs into the legislature. Each MPP represents a specific area of the province and is responsible for raising the concerns of the people from his or her riding to the other MPPs.

The Premier, or the leader of the Ontario political party who was elected by Ontarians, also works from Queen's Park. His or her job is to oversee the provincial government and set goals for the other members to follow. The Lieutenant-Governor and the Cabinet Ministers work at Queen's Park too. The provincial government is responsible for making decisions related to education, health care, and the police.

R r

The Rideau Canal is a man-made canal that stretches from Ottawa to Kingston. It is about 278 kilometres long. The Canal was originally built by the British after the War of 1812 to serve as a safe supply route from Montreal to Kingston. Today the Rideau Canal attracts thousands of tourists to Ottawa, the capital city of Canada, every year. People come to the Canal to take part in boating, sailing, and a variety of festivals that are celebrated on or near the Rideau Canal throughout the year. During the winter the canal is used for skating. Every February, Winterlude, North America's greatest winter festival, is celebrated for two weeks. The portion of the Rideau Canal that is located in Ottawa is transformed into the world's longest skating rink! It is about 7.8 kilometres. long. The rink is opened daily for other activities too such as hockey, curling, and exhibitions by world figure skating champions.

Skating, boating, and sailing
are things to do on R.
The Rideau Canal of Ottawa
attracts tourists from near and far.

Today when you hear the name Laura Secord you probably think of the chocolate company named after our great heroine. Do you know of Laura Secord's brave actions during the War of 1812? She ran approximately 30 kilometres to warn the British army of an American attack. This attack on the British could have led the Americans to control the Niagara Peninsula and the Horseshoe Falls. Due to Laura's bravery, both remained a part of Upper Canada.

Laura Secord settled in Upper Canada in a town called Queenston with her husband. Queenston still remains a town in the Niagara region today. The Secord family home has been restored and made into a museum. A monument also stands in a churchyard in Niagara Falls in memory of Laura Secord.

S also stands for the Stratford Festival of Canada. First established in 1953 as a festival based on Shakespeare's plays, the festival has grown to include many other productions and has become a world class theatrical producer. Many internationally acclaimed actors have performed at the Stratford Festival over the years.

S s

S is for our heroine—
Laura Secord is her name.
It was the braveness of her actions
that brought her glory and fame.

Tt

Also named as the province's symbol, the white trillium became the provincial flower in 1937. Its white petals are a symbol for peace and hope. Found in forests throughout the province during the spring, the white trillium is easily recognized. The plant has three pointed green leaves and one white, three-petaled flower. When the trillium gets older, it turns pink.

The white trillium is a beautiful flower; however, it should never be picked. Conservationists protect the trillium in its natural environment because it takes many years for the trillium to bloom again once it has been cut from its root or stem.

T can also stand for Toronto, the capital city of Ontario. More than 60 cultures are represented in Toronto. The United Nations has named Toronto as the most culturally diverse city in the world. Downtown Toronto is also the home of the CN Tower, which is the tallest building in the world, measuring 553.33 metres in height.

T is for Trillium,
protected and white.
Ontario's flower
is a breathtaking sight.

U is for Upper Canada,
a British Colony way back when.
In 1867 it became Ontario,
one province out of ten.

Upper Canada, an early name for Ontario, was created by the Constitutional Act of 1791. The area was called Upper Canada from 1791 until 1841. A lot of Ontario's heritage can be traced back to this time period. In 1791 about 10,000 people lived in Upper Canada. Most of these people were United Empire Loyalists, or people who chose to stay loyal to England. Part of the population was also made up of Francophone and Aboriginal people. In 1841 Upper and Lower Canada became a province of Canada. At the time the area was renamed Canada West. Ontario and Quebec then became separate provinces in 1867. These two provinces joined Nova Scotia and New Brunswick to form a federal union, the Dominion of Canada. This is when Ottawa was named Canada's capital city and Sir John A. Macdonald became the first prime minister of the country. Today Ontario is one of ten Canadian provinces and three territories.

U u

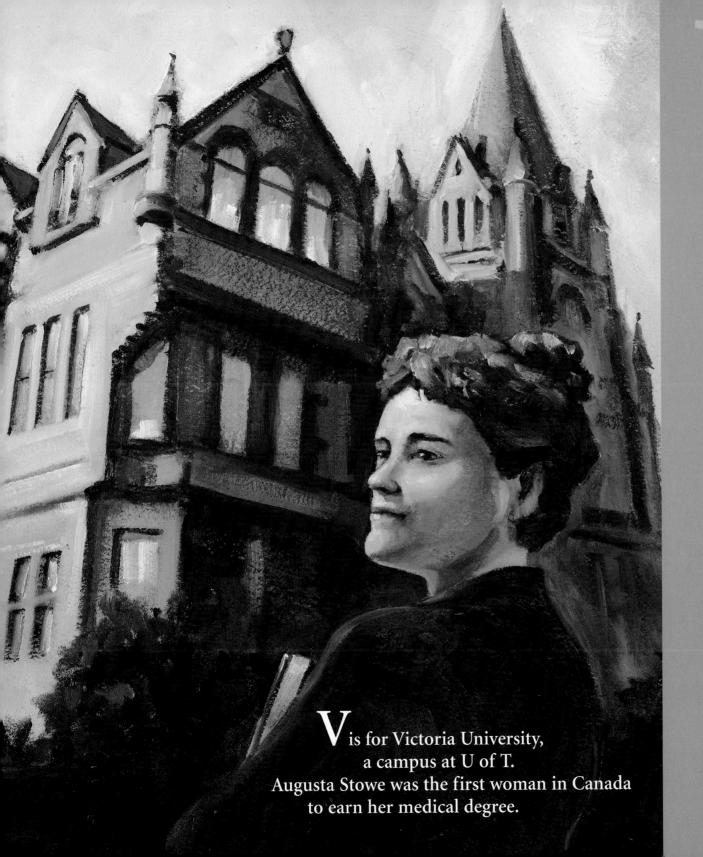

V is for Victoria University,
a campus at U of T.
Augusta Stowe was the first woman in Canada
to earn her medical degree.

Victoria University is a part of the University of Toronto, which is one of Canada's top schools and the largest university in Canada. "Vic", as it is called, is made up of Victoria College and Emmanuel College. The campus is located across from Queen's Park in Toronto. The university was originally founded in Cobourg, Ontario, then moved to Toronto in 1892. When the school was located in Cobourg, Augusta Stowe attended the Faculty of Medicine at Victoria University. In 1883 she became the first woman to graduate from an Ontario university and the first woman to receive a Canadian medical degree.

Ontario has other famous women who were the first to accomplish many great things. Some of these women include: Emily Stowe, who was Augusta's mother, earned her medical degree in the United States and was the first woman to practice medicine in Canada; Marilyn Bell, from Toronto, the first person to swim across Lake Ontario in 1954; and Roberta Bondar, from Sault Ste. Marie, the first Canadian woman to travel into space.

Wis for Wikwemikong Pow Wow—
come see all the celebrations.
Dances, songs, and stories told
by people of our First Nations.

The Wikwemikong Pow Wow is one of the largest and longest running Pow Wows in North America. Approximately 250 dancers and singers and over 55 food and craft vendors get together for this spectacular native celebration every first weekend of August on Manitoulin Island. The island has a large First Nations population and is the largest freshwater island in the world. People from across Canada and the United States gather to celebrate through a variety of dance and drumming events as they compete for prizes.

W also stands for Windsor, the automotive capital of Canada. It is the most southern city in the country. The Ambassador Bridge, North America's number one international border crossing for goods traded between Canada and the United States, is found here.

W
W

Locally known as "The Ex," the Canadian National Exhibition first opened on September 3, 1879. Located on Toronto's waterfront, the fair was then named the Toronto Industrial Exhibition. The success of the first fair led to the annual operation of the C. N. E. The fair's name was changed in 1904 and promoted agriculture, horticulture, arts, and industry. Today the Ex runs from late August until Labour Day weekend (the first Monday of September). There are over 500 attractions, 700 exhibitors, and 65 rides. The Conklin Midway and the Food Building are popular attractions for many visitors. Horse shows, the Air Show, international exhibits, and horticultural displays are just some of the many events that take place every summer at the C. N. E. The Exhibition has grown a great deal over the years and is now recognized as the world's largest annual exposition.

X
x

The C. N. E. can be for X,
called the "Ex" by you and me.
The Canadian National Exhibition—
so many things to do and see!

Yy

"Yours to discover"
is the phrase we'll use for Y.
It's seen on all licence plates
of vehicles passing by.

Ontario licence plates are used to identify all vehicles driven in the province. The licence plate allows people to drive on roads in Ontario. Licence plates are sold to people or companies throughout the province. Many types of licence plates are issued in Ontario. These include: Passenger, Commercial, Trailer, Bus, School Bus, Motorcycle, Dealer, Diplomatic, Farm, Off Road Vehicle, and Snowmobile. Passenger vehicles, such as cars, have white Ontario plates with blue lettering. Ontario plates for commercial vehicles are white with black lettering.

Y also stands for Yonge Street, the longest street in the world! Yonge Street measures almost 1,900 kilometres. in length. It stretches from Lake Ontario all the way to the town of Rainy River in Ontario. The street has been the main street of Toronto since the late eighteenth century and has undergone many changes.

Zinc is mined in our province,
a mineral to use for Z.
Deposits are found in the north
along with nickel, gold, and lead.

Today Ontario is one of the world's top 10 producers of minerals. Canada sells Ontario's minerals and the metals made from them to several other countries around the world. Ontario is especially rich in minerals such as zinc, nickel, copper, and lead. Zinc, which is mined in Timmins and Thunder Bay, has many uses. It can be mixed with copper to produce brass or used as a protective coating for steel. In the 1960s, large deposits of zinc and copper were found near Timmins. This mining town is also an important gold mining centre in Ontario. Thunder Bay is rich in other natural resources like gold, copper, lead, and amethyst, Ontario's provincial mineral.

Large deposits of nickel are mined in Sudbury. When travelling through Sudbury, Canada's mining centre, one must stop to see the nine metre tall Big Nickel. This famous tourist attraction is a monument to the Canadian nickel industry.

Z z

More Facts to Discover

1. Who was Tom Thomson?

2. When did the Common Loon become Ontario's provincial bird?

3. What is the seventh Natural Wonder of the World?

4. What is Ontario's provincial mineral?

5. Name the longest street in the world.

6. Who was the most important Father of Confederation?

7. What was Henry Hudson hoping to discover in 1609?

8. Name Canada's oldest provincial park.

9. What does the white trillium symbolize?

10. Frederick Banting and Charles Best made an extremely important discovery at the University of Toronto. What was this discovery and when was it made?

11. Where did Alexander Graham Bell make his first long distance telephone call?

12. What is the largest freshwater island in the world? What event takes place on this island every summer?

13. Where are Ontario laws discussed and passed?

14. What does the Rideau Canal become in the winter?

15. What is the largest physical region in Canada?

16. Name the four Great Lakes that border Ontario.

Answers

1. The artist who inspired The Group of Seven
2. June 23, 1994.
3. Niagara Falls
4. Amethyst
5. Yonge Street
6. Sir John A. Macdonald
7. The Northwest Passage to Asia
8. Algonquin Park
9. Peace and hope
10. Insulin, between 1921 and 1922
11. Brantford, Ontario
12. Manitoulin Island, The Wikwemikong Pow Wow
13. Queen's Park
14. The world's longest skating rink
15. The Canadian Shield
16. Lake Ontario, Erie, Huron, Superior

Other Ontario Fun Facts

Did you know that Ontario has many professional sports teams? Some of them include: The Toronto Blue Jays, The Hamilton Tiger-Cats, The Ottawa Senators, The Toronto Maple Leafs, The Toronto Raptors, The Ottawa Renegades, and The Toronto Argonauts. Do you know the sport each of these teams play?

Paramount Canada's Wonderland, located in Vaughan, Ontario, is Canada's premier theme park with nine themed areas and over 200 attractions!

If you look at a map of Ontario, the outline of the province looks like an elephant. Try it out!

Shania Twain, world famous country and pop singer, was born in Timmins, Ontario.

Some popular Hollywood stars lived in Ontario. Mike Myers grew up in Scarborough, and Jim Carrey was born in Newmarket.

Lovenia Gorman

Lovenia Gorman was born in Toronto, Ontario, where she currently resides with her husband, Andrew, and their children, Alexandra and Sawyer. Lovenia is an elementary school teacher who works for the Toronto District School Board. *A is for Algonquin: An Ontario Alphabet* is the first book she has written. When not teaching, Lovenia spends summers operating her children's art camp, enjoying time with family and friends, and visiting Algonquin Park.

Melanie Rose

Melanie Rose was born in England and immigrated to Canada as a child. A graduate of the Ontario College of Art, she has lived in Ontario for 16 years. She currently lives in Mississauga with her son, Liam, and her two cats, Mickey and Meesha. *A is for Algonquin: An Ontario Alphabet* is Melanie's 7th book with Sleeping Bear Press.